LOOKING UP IN

LONDON AS YOU HAVE NEVE ... BEFORE

JANE PEYTON

Photographs by Helen Peyton

WILEY-ACADEMY

For my family, with love

Published in Great Britain in 2003 by Wiley-Academy, a division of John Wiley & Sons Ltd

Email (for orders and customer service enquiries): cs-books@wiley.co.uk
Visit our Home Page on www.wileyeurope.com or www.wiley.com

Other Wiley Editorial Offices

John Wiley & Sons Inc., 111 River Street, Hoboken, NJ 07030, USA
Jossey-Bass, 989 Market Street, San Francisco, CA 94103-1741, USA
Wiley-VCH Verlag GmbH, Boschstr. 12, D-69469 Weinheim, Germany
John Wiley & Sons Australia Ltd, 33 Park Road, Milton, Queensland 4064, Australia
John Wiley & Sons (Asia) Pte Ltd, 2 Clementi Loop #02-01, Jin Xing Distripark, Singapore 129809
John Wiley & Sons Canada Ltd, 22 Worcester Road, Etobicoke, Ontario, Canada M9W 1L1

ISBN 0470849428

Cover design: Artmedia Press Ltd, London
Text design: Liz Brown
Maps: Louisa Fitch
Typeset by Atelier Data Services, St Austell, Cornwall, UK

Printed and bound in Italy

CONTENTS

PREFACE

Warning! Reading this book will change your habits. Compiling *Looking up in London* has changed mine. I find it impossible to travel anywhere now without tilting my head and looking up at the facades of the buildings. When I lived overseas I had to drive a convertible car to indulge my obsession. Now I live in London, I travel everywhere by bicycle. I secretly cheer when the traffic lights are on red so I can stop and look at the buildings around me. Travelling on the Underground is out of the question. I occasionally take a bus, sitting on the upper deck, ideally an open-topped one.

Exploring almost any street in London reveals a seemingly endless range of splendid architectural details. Standing on Waterloo Bridge, looking east and west along the river offers a spectacular view of the city and makes me want to investigate its ancient thoroughfares to find new treasures above eye level.

Working with my sister as her camera assistant was a hoot. The job was a mixture of tea lady, porter and safety officer. It involved finding the best takeaway cafés; holding onto the boss's legs to prevent her falling as she leaned over a fence to get a perfect shot; spreading newspaper on the ground for her to lie upon to find the best photographic angle and shouting warnings as she crouched in the middle of a busy road searching for the best frame.

When the photographs were developed and friends looked at them, they were amazed to see a London they did not recognize, despite having lived in the city for years. This confirmed for me the concept of the book: that because people rarely look above eye level in the street, when they do, it is like visiting a new place, or certainly a different dimension of something familiar.

From a list of hundreds of locations, I reluctantly slashed it to 64. I was searching for diverse architectural features that would take readers around a wide swathe of Central London. Unfortunately London south of the river is barely represented in the book. Several locations in Southwark that I had planned to include were being refurbished when the photographs were shot and were covered in scaffolding. I combed the streets looking for other great locations, but in my opinion, unimaginative post-war development south of the river has left the real gems surrounded by ugliness and I did not want to strand readers in an area without something beautiful to look at.

My choice of sites is subjective, facades that

caught my eye and made me stop to look closer. In many cases, although a building as a whole was stunning, trying to isolate a small part of it did not make a satisfactory photograph so reluctantly I disregarded it. Location also influenced my choice. I did not choose sites that were too far from the suggested route, or that isolated readers in a part of London with little else to look at. This book is just a taster of the hundreds of buildings waiting to be discovered by you.

I am particularly grateful to Tony Harman of Maple Leaf Images, Skipton, North Yorkshire, who generously lent us his camera equipment and developed the photographs with such great care.

Maggie Toy, Senior Commissioning Editor at John Wiley, thank you for believing in the concept of *Looking up in London* and pulling my initial outline from your big pile of unsolicited manuscripts.

Thank you to all the archivists, building services managers, marketing and publicity professionals who supplied historical information about the buildings featured in the book.

Martin Barrell, Nicole Cantu, Janet Fitch, Emily Fitch, Louisa Fitch, Lilian Humphrays, Michael Moseley, Emma Robertshaw, Amanda Sellers, Anne Simmonds, Mark Simmonds, Nick Smith, Colin Woodhead, Lindy Woodhead – thank you for your generosity, kindness, support, creative suggestions. Gail Willumsen who was my unofficial editor, and helped me to improve my prose, thank you. And to all the friends who have ever fed or watered me, cheers!

Jane Peyton

PLAYING THE LOOKING UP IN LONDON GAME

Your mission, if you choose to accept it, is to explore the architectural treasures featured in this book. Imagine you are a detective and put your best sleuthing foot forward. You are on a journey to discover the incredible buildings that combine to make London such a fascinating and beautiful city.

This book is the key to a secret London. It will enable you to see the city as the people who scurry along streets looking straight ahead do not. Entering London's hidden world is simple, just look up above eye level and prepare for a surprise. Giants, gargoyles and gods are gazing down, waiting to be admired.

The tour begins in the oldest neighbourhood of London, known as the City of London (or The City), and it directs readers through eleven districts of central London. Along the route are the architectural gems in the photographs. Your goal is to find them, using the book as a guide.

To assist you in the assignment, simple maps of the locales are provided.

You are supplied with three clues about each mystery site.

1./ The street name on which it is located

2./ A map grid

3./ A cryptic clue about the location, or its vicinity.

Arm yourself with a detailed map of central London and slip on some comfortable footwear. Once you are on the route, choose a photograph and start looking up until you spot the gem shown. To learn more about the site, turn the page for a brief introduction to its history.

Do not be confused in the few instances where the street address in the clue differs from the official postal address. This happens occasionally with large structures such as the Bank of England that has facades on several streets.

Where the answer to the cryptic clue is not apparent in the location's description, it is explained.

If sleuthing is not your style, you can still explore London above eye level using the book as a straightforward travel guide. Just look overleaf of the photograph for the exact street address of the location.

To be honest, your mission will never be complete. Once you start looking up, you will be unable to stop, no matter where you are.

INTRODUCTION: LONDON'S FIRST TWO MILLENNIA

Vacant Green Field Site With Development Potential: London in Roman Times

Location, location, location. That's what real estate agents believe and the Romans believed it too. In AD43, they picked a prime spot to found a minor military garrison called Londinium. Situated on the banks of an estuarine river (later known as the Thames) at a point where it could easily be crossed, Londinium was a lay-by on a network of military roads that connected major Roman towns such as St Albans and Colchester. Britain was an unfriendly place for Romans to be stationed, with hostile Celtic tribes who called Britain home, mounting regular attacks on the invaders. It was also an inhospitable land to the Romans, with none of the creature comforts they took for granted. Londinium's direct link along the River Thames to the North Sea was paramount therefore, because it meant crucial provisions such as wine and olive oil could be imported from the civilized world.

Londinium's earliest buildings were constructed with a framework of twigs held together by clay plaster, also known as wattle and daub. But only 17 years after the founding of the settlement, the Romans would come to regret the flammable nature of their buildings. In AD60, Boudicca – Queen of a Celtic tribe, the Iceni – and her followers charged into Londinium and burned it to the ground in revenge against the Romans for enslaving the women and children of their tribe. By now, Londinium's strategic significance was apparent to the Romans and the settlement was reconstructed, this time in stone and with new prominence as the capital of Roman Britain. The colonizers were there to stay. New Londinium was more like a Roman town with a basilica, assembly rooms, temples, a forum, administrative buildings, public baths and palaces.

For a sense of how people lived in the capital almost 2000 years ago, take a trip to the Museum of London where Roman artefacts bring the ancient town to life.

Boudicca had taught the Romans a lesson, so they built a defensive stone wall, parts of which can still be seen today, most notably at Tower Hill. But Britain's angry Celts could not be subdued and by AD410, the Emperor Honorious decided to cut his losses and withdrew all military forces. The Roman era in Britain was over.

Tenants Sought For Abandoned Property: Saxon London

Britons waving goodbye and good riddance to the Roman soldiers had little time to celebrate when the Saxons, a Teutonic tribe from what is now Germany, arrived to claim the capital. The Saxons dominated Britain for the next few hundred years but there is little written history or physical evidence of their tenancy of the country during the Dark Ages.

Historical records show that the Saxons established a settlement outside the city walls in what is now Aldwych and Covent Garden. They named it Lundenwic – *wic* is a Saxon word meaning 'marketplace'. Saxon buildings bore no resemblance to the Roman style. They were simple square or rectangular structures of wood and thatch or moss with packed earth floors that simply vanished over time, providing archaeologists with few architectural traces of the early period of Saxon occupation.

Though they did not excel at creating lasting monuments, the Saxons were master craftsmen, as the jewellery excavated at the burial site in Sutton Hoo attests. On display at the British Museum, treasures such as a magnificent gold belt buckle worked with interlaced ribbons and tiny animal heads suggest that the Saxons were the Tiffany & Co. of their day.

By AD804, London was once again a bustling trading town, according to the writings of the Venerable Bede, a monk. A blessing and a curse, the River Thames was good for trade but bad for the enemy invaders it bore right into the capital. From the 9th century, Britain was invaded several times by fierce warriors from Scandinavia, the Danes, a.k.a. the Vikings. Hundreds of their ships sailed up the Thames in AD851 and the Vikings laid waste to London, burning the city and murdering anyone who had not already fled. Sixteen years later, the Danes returned for good, to set up a military garrison in a city resurrected from the ruins of their own destruction.

The Viking's tenancy of London was more like a time-share. The Saxons were no pushovers and mounted a spirited attack under the leadership of King Alfred. After three years of laying siege to the city, Alfred was at last victorious when the enemy sued for peace.

Alfred had earned his sobriquet 'The Great' and instituted a programme of rebuilding in London, subdividing the city in patterns that dictate the street layout to this day. A major beneficiary of Alfred's generous land allocation was the Catholic Church: great monasteries and priories were established. The King also ordered the city wall to be fortified. Thanks to his foresight, sporadic Viking raids were, in the main, repelled.

The Danes were nothing if not determined however, and in 1013, after a long siege, once again they took possession of London.

The ousted Saxon King Aethelred was having none of this and he took flight to continental Europe. For months he worked to gather military support for the liberation of London. Under orders from King Olaf of Norway, a fleet of Norse ships set out on a mission to rout the Vikings from London. The ships sailed up the Thames and tethered with ropes to the wooden posts of London Bridge. As the tide ebbed, the ropes dislodged the support posts and the entire bridge tumbled into the river, providing the theme of the song 'London Bridge is falling down.' Londoners thanked the Norse King (who was later beatified for his devout Christianity) by naming several churches after him. Only one of them survives, St. Olave, Hart Street.

Despite many years of Danish occupation of London, the Danes made no permanent mark on the architecture of the city. That accolade was to go to a minor aristocrat on the other side of the English Channel.

Must See – Cutting Edge Architecture: Norman London

Wealthy Britain was a sitting target for opportunists seeking to enrich themselves, and William, Duke of Normandy was one of them. He raised an army, sailed across the English Channel from France and landed on England's southern shores in 1066. The Battle of Hastings ensued, with the English King, Harold leading his troops against the invaders. It was to no avail, Harold was killed in battle and the Norman army was victorious. William proclaimed himself King and set his army to ravage the country and to quash any insurrection. The new King wisely spared the capital the violence wrought elsewhere because he needed the wealth of the city traders. William's invasion of England was the beginning of the Norman period, an era of stability that saw London's population increase and the city flourish as an international trading centre.

To send his new subjects a visual signal of his military power, William the Conqueror (as he came to be known) ordered the construction of an imposing defensive structure called the White Tower. It was the first example of Romanesque architecture in Britain. Although much altered today, it can still be seen within the Tower of London. The Norman period was associated with Romanesque architecture, characterized by heavy stone structures with rounded arches and circular pillars. For the majority of Londoners, homes and businesses were still constructed of wood and thatch, with stone reserved for only the wealthiest of citizens. Typically, houses in London were crammed closely together on the narrow streets, with commercial activities on the ground floor and accommodation above.

With the Normans came the end of a thousand years of invasions. There was a sense of peace and Londoners were able to concentrate on building the city into a trading giant. They may no longer have quaked at the thought of enemy attack but their lives were still dominated, though this time it was by men in black.

For Sale – Extensive Properties. One Respectable Owner: Medieval and Tudor London

The Catholic Church wielded immense influence during the medieval era. With its vast wealth and land holdings, the Church packed the city with monasteries, convents and associated buildings. All over London, great stone churches arose, places of worship that praised God while reminding the congregation of the Church's power. Ancient street names still in use today are a reminder of the ubiquity of Church establishments – Austin Friars Passage, Allhallows Lane, Priory Court.

In the 12th century, the Church abandoned the Romanesque style for the new Gothic architecture with its pointed arches, narrow walls and soaring towers. Westminster Abbey is the epitome of Gothic architecture.

Medieval London was alive with commerce – livestock in Smithfield; produce markets at Eastcheap and Cheapside; wool weaving; tailoring; tanning; metal working. Hundreds of tiny shops lined London's streets and dozens of wharves along the riverbank handled all manner of goods: spices from the Spice Islands, incense from the Red Sea, wine from France.

But even the mightiest institution can topple from power. In 1536 the Catholic Church refused to countenance the divorce of King Henry VIII from Catherine of Aragon. Henry's response was devastating. He formally broke away from the Church of Rome and declared himself the Head of the Church of England. In one bold stroke, he stripped the Catholic Church of its influence and assets. In an act known as the 'Dissolution of the Monasteries', Henry took possession of the Church's vast wealth of land and property throughout the country.

What Henry did not retain for the Crown, he sold or gave as gifts to favourites. The release of land in London into private ownership led to developments of housing and commercial buildings, which increased the size of the city. The plunder had no end: even the stones from priories and churches were looted by Henry's courtiers and used to build their palatial homes outside the city walls along what is now Strand.

As London's fortune grew, country-folk flocked to the city, and the population exploded. Wealthy citizens could afford mansions outside the defensive walls but, for most Londoners, simply surviving in the city was a challenge. Streets were crowded with high-density housing and filth was everywhere. Excrement ran down open channels in the middle of thoroughfares. Butchers tossed the innards of slaughtered animals into the street. The stench of rotting food filled the air. London became a perfect haven for rats and for plague.

Plague was first recorded in London in *AD*664 and over the centuries it claimed hundreds of thousands of lives in dozens of outbreaks. One outbreak in particular captures the imagination: the Black Death of 1348. The epidemic was out of control in the crowded living conditions of the medieval city. In certain streets there was no one left alive to bury the dead. London's last big incidence of plague, known as the Great Plague, in 1665 was followed a year later by another devastating event. Fire.

Special Offer – Fixer Uppers. Some Fire Damage: Stuart, Jacobean and Georgian London

There were no emergency services to call on the night of September 2nd 1666 when fire broke out in a baker's premises on Pudding Lane. Strong winds fanned the flames and in the following four days they destroyed 80 percent of the city. London's predominantly wooden buildings became nothing but tinder. Few lives were lost but the fire consumed historic churches, livery halls and thousands of houses. The majority of Tudor buildings built during the reigns of King Henry VIII and Queen Elizabeth were destroyed. One remains, though much restored, in High Holborn. Staples Inn with its timber frame, white plaster and leaden-paned windows typifies buildings from medieval times and hints of what London streets looked like over 500 years ago.

After the fire, architects such as Christopher Wren rebuilt the city. Wren envisaged a London of wide tree-lined boulevards. His grand vision came to nothing, however, because the system of piecemeal land ownership established by King Alfred was so complicated. Over the years, land in London had been divided and subdivided. Property that belonged to the monasteries had been taken by the Crown or sold. London was owned by many landlords and trying to persuade them to accept the new city plans would have involved lengthy negotiations. Pressure to rebuild quickly meant the London that rose from the ashes followed the pre-fire street patterns.

Strict building codes decreed that no wooden structures were permitted. The dominant new construction material was brick and London took on a sienna hue.

Plague and fire had led the wealthy to settle in the newer parts of London – Westminster, Bloomsbury, Soho – while the poor remained in the cramped living conditions of the old city. Greater London continued to expand north and west, to St James's, Kensington and Marylebone. These fashionable areas were among the first to feature terraced brick houses built around leafy squares, quiet streets and gracious crescents, still a characteristic of urban London today.

At the dawn of the Georgian era (1714), the dominant architectural style was Neo-Classical, influenced by Ancient Greek and Roman buildings. Under-statement characterized Georgian architectural taste. New urban developments like Covent Garden reflected a style known as Palladian, after the Italian architect Andrea Palladio, who advocated symmetrical buildings with facades resembling Greek or Roman temples. Spencer House in Green Park is considered a fine example of Palladianism. Even today parts of inner London are overwhelmingly Classical. Walking late at night through the squares in Bloomsbury, without the noise and traffic of the modern city, one can almost imagine the London of three centuries ago.

In 1801, the city's first population census recorded one million inhabitants and London gained new fame as the world's largest city. This exalted status was expressed in a flurry of splendid new public buildings: the National Gallery, British Museum, University of London (now University College) and St George's Hospital at Hyde Park Corner (now the Lanesborough Hotel). Greek Revival architecture was popular at the beginning of the 19th century. Fashionable developments in the neighbourhoods of Pimlico and Belgravia adhered to this style, with rows of cream stucco houses fronted by porticoes and columns as far as the eye could see.

Early in the 19th century, new bridges at Waterloo, Vauxhall and Southwark made vast tracts of land south of the river ripe for development. Southwark was a settlement on the other side of London Bridge that was founded by the Romans at the same time as Londinium. By the 17th century it was the second largest urban centre in England. Pre-eminent in trade, Southwark's riverfront was lined with wharves and warehouses where tons of international wares were handled. Southwark also became known as a reveller's playground with its brothels, bear-baiting spectacles, raucous pubs and theatres, including the Rose and Globe where

Shakespeare and Marlowe's works were performed. Southwark's streets, just as those of its neighbour across the river, were narrow and crammed with wooden buildings. And just like its neighbour, Southwark had its own devastating conflagration 10 years after London's Great Fire.

The Industrial Revolution (from the mid-18th century onwards) transformed Britain forever from a rural society to a nation of town-dwellers. Most of the new urban population had come to the capital in the belief that 'London's streets are paved with gold'. In order to accommodate its new inhabitants, London was about to change again.

Compulsory Purchase Order – Redevelopment Coming Soon: Victorian London

During the Victorian era (beginning in 1837) mass transit was introduced to London. Railways, omnibuses and later the Underground spurred the development of suburbs, and the city spread over an even larger area. People continued to pour into the capital for the opportunities it afforded but many of the new arrivals were destitute and joined other paupers in the slums of the city, straining the already over-stretched infrastructure. Faced with frequent outbreaks of cholera and typhoid, Victorian governments made a major issue of sanitation in the capital. The Thames was an open cesspool for the city until 1858, the year of 'The Great Stink' when the stench from the river overwhelmed politicians sitting in the Houses of Parliament, and prompted construction of the extensive sewer system that still carries London's waste. Land was reclaimed from the river and the main sewer was built under what is today the Victoria Embankment. This explains why the Strand no longer abuts the river. In a campaign to improve sanitary conditions, acres of slums were razed. Unfortunately in their zeal, city officials demolished countless historical structures which explains why there are more Victorian public buildings in Central London than of any other era. Stylistically, Gothic Revival is most associated with the Victorians: the Houses of Parliament are a supreme example.

The Victorians had made an indelible mark on the architecture of the city, just as their immediate successors were to do.

Modern City Of Diverse Architecture: London in the 20th century

With the death Queen Victoria in 1901, an era came to an end. By now, 4.5 million people lived in London and the city spread in all directions. Adjacent villages became suburbs of Greater London. The city was the commercial capital of the world and London was the centre of a huge empire. Britain's Imperial might and confidence were reflected in a commanding style of architecture known as Edwardian Baroque. It was the choice for public buildings such as the headquarters of the London County Council – now a hotel and aquarium – standing on the south bank of the Thames opposite the Houses of Parliament. With its decorative ornamentation, Victoria Station's edifice is also a good example of the grand visual statements that Baroque brought to London.

In the 1920s and 30s, the Art Deco style made a limited impact on the city. Compared to Baroque, Art Deco was understated and simple, with smooth uncluttered surfaces and curved corners. A black glass building in Fleet Street, near Ludgate Circus personifies this style. The discovery of King Tutankhamen's tomb in 1922 led to Egyptomania. A careful look above eye level reveals carvings, details and bas-reliefs influenced by the discovery of the boy king's tomb.

During World War II, the Nazis bombed London. The City and the East End where the docks and industry were centred were especially devastated. For eight months starting in September 1940, bombs rained from the sky. In one period, Londoners endured 57 consecutive nights of bombing raids. A famous photograph of the time shows St Paul's Cathedral surrounded by smoke as the buildings in the immediate vicinity burn. Miraculously, the Cathedral was unharmed. The human toll was terrible, however; more than 15,000 Londoners lost their lives during the Blitz.

After the war, lack of money and imagination led to bombsites being replaced by hastily built, functional buildings that did not complement their historical neighbours. A particularly heinous eyesore was the Paternoster Square development that spoiled the approach to St Paul's Cathedral. Forty years after construction, Paternoster Square is gone, and a new development harmonises with the Baroque splendour of St Paul's Cathedral.

The post-war years were austere. Rationing continued until the mid-1950s and the country struggled to recover physically and mentally. There was nothing playful about the architecture of the South Bank centre where new concert halls and theatres were built for the 1951 Festival of Britain in place of the bomb-damaged acres south of the river. Its windowless boxes, concrete walls and forbidding windswept walkways came to embody a type of architecture known as 'Brutalism'. This sterile but economical style satisfied the urgent need to build accommodation for the thousands who had lost their homes during the war. Practicality would reign over aesthetics and soon hundreds of bleak high-rise public housing blocks punctuated the London skyline.

In the 1960s, a property boom led to an explosion of quickly constructed unimaginative office buildings. An increase in the birth rate led to an urgent demand for new homes and block upon block of ugly public housing developments blighted London's suburbs.

Since the 1980s, a renewed appreciation for design and style is revitalizing the city. Now there is great prestige in retaining leading architects to create buildings that make a statement or complement the urban landscape. No single style of architecture dominates. Some recent buildings look forward, like Lloyds of London in Leadenhall Street, or backwards, like the London Underwriting Centre near Fenchurch Street that resembles a gigantic medieval Gothic church.

Since the turn of the Millennium, property prices in London, both commercial and residential, are at an all-time high and yet there has been a frenzy of building: a fitting tribute to a great city that continues to flourish after nearly 2000 years.

The City of London

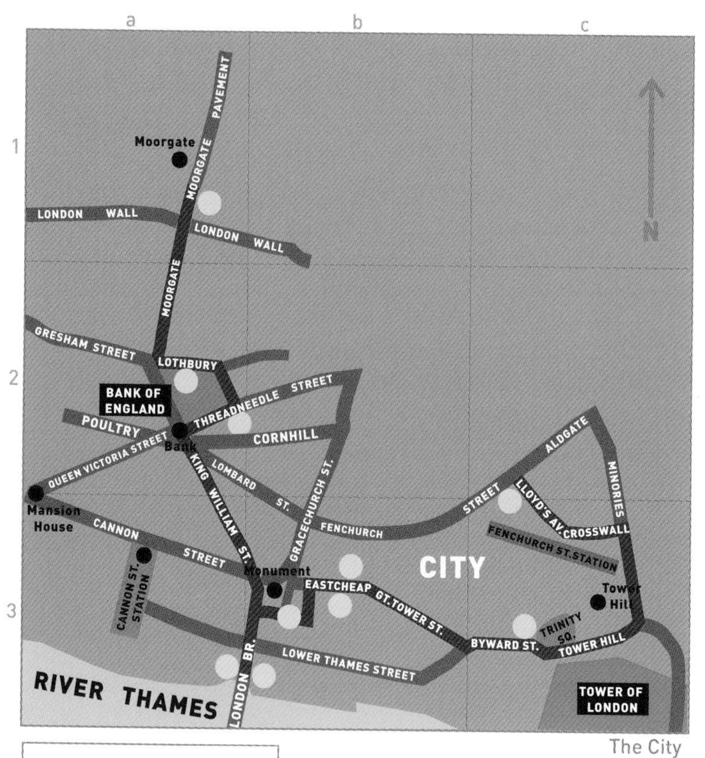

The City

WALKING ROUTE

MAJOR STREETS

LOCATION OF PHOTOGRAPH

LONDON UNDERGROUND STATION

MAJOR LANDMARK

PARKS & OPEN SPACES

Location:	Fenchurch St, EC3. South side of the street
Map Grid:	2c
Tube station:	Tower Hill
Bus route:	15, 25, 78, 100
Architect:	Thomas Colcutt
Built:	1899–1901
Style:	French Renaissance
Cryptic clue:	Welsh surname of the bank and the insurer

Address

Lloyd's Register, 71 Fenchurch Street, EC3

Naked sea nymphs, sea monsters and seahorses decorate the ornate facade of Lloyd's Register. The nymphs sit demurely while the monsters and seahorses cavort in the waves. Heavily laden ships, and maidens bearing maritime instruments flank the Greek god Hermes, the protector of travellers. The nautical themes are appropriate given the purpose of Lloyd's Register. Founded in 1760 by customers of Lloyd's Coffee House, the Register's original aim was to provide underwriters and merchants with information about the condition of ships being chartered or insured.

The 'Lloyd's Register Lady' featured in the photograph is one of several decorative shields on the building's gates.

Location:	Trinity Square, EC3. West side of the square
Map grid:	3c
Tube station:	Tower Hill
Bus route:	15, 25, 78, 100
Architect:	Edwin Cooper
Built:	1912–22
Style:	Edwardian Baroque
Cryptic clue:	Patriarch of London's river

10 Trinity Square, EC3

Father Thames surveys the river from a building that formerly housed the Port of London Authority. Without the river, London might not have been settled so it is fair to say that the Thames is the father *and* mother of the city.

Roman general Julius Caesar who visited the area in 51BC referred to the river as Tamesis. Caesar was on an exploratory mission to look for territory to claim for the Roman Empire. Saxon names for the river included *Temis* and *Temes.*

Trinity Square has a gruesome past. Until 1780, it was the setting for public executions. Many Londoners enjoyed a day out to watch an execution. Depending on the popularity of the condemned, the executioner was loudly cheered or booed by the crowd as he practised his craft. An unobtrusive memorial in the square marks the spot where 125 enemies of the Crown were beheaded.

Location:	Eastcheap, EC3. North side of the street
Map grid:	3b
Tube station:	Tower Hill or Monument
Bus route:	15, 17, 25, 48, 133, 344
Architect:	Robert Lewis Roumieu
Built:	1868
Style:	Gothic
Cryptic clue:	Multiply the Little Pigs by 11

33 Eastcheap, EC3

William Shakespeare was a customer at the Boar's Head tavern on Eastcheap, and it is mentioned in the play Henry IV part II. The Boar's Head was located at what is now 33 Eastcheap. This explains the carving of the boar in the photograph. The tavern was destroyed during the Great Fire of London but was rebuilt. It continued with its rowdy reputation until the owner, suddenly reformed, gave the tavern to a local church.

The Boar's Head was demolished in the 19th century to make way for the building in the photograph.

Location:	20 Eastcheap EC3. South side of the street
Map Grid:	3b
Tube station:	Tower Hill or Monument
Bus route:	15, 17, 25, 48, 133, 344
Architect:	Alexander Peebles. Relief by William Theed
Built:	1883–5
Style:	Victorian
Cryptic clue:	Hotel Sierra Bravo Charlie

HSBC, Peek House, 20 Eastcheap, EC3

Prostitutes were so busy working on the street next to Peek House that it was known from medieval times as Love Lane. This reminder of its colourful past was lost when Love Lane was renamed in 1939. Lovat Lane was chosen in honour of Lord Lovat whose fisheries annually provided tonnes of salmon to the nearby Billingsgate fish market.

The camel train in the photograph may be carrying tea, for Peek House was the London offices of tea merchant Peek Brothers.

Eastcheap, first recorded in 1100 was for centuries the
ncipal market of London. *Chepe* was an old English word
g 'market'. Excavations during the 19th century
Roman road three feet below the current street
level.

Cryptic Clue explanation: Hotel Sierra Bravo Charlie is part of the phonetic alphabet and stands for HSBC.

Location:	Fish St Hill, EC3. Centre of the street
Map Grid:	3b
Tube station:	Monument
Bus route:	15, 17, 25, 48, 133, 344
Architect:	Christopher Wren and Robert Hooke
Built:	1671–7
Style:	Doric column
Cryptic clue:	A monumental structure in memory of the flames

Monument, Monument Street, EC3

There are fires and there are *fires*. The Great Fire of London was one of the latter. So much so, the Monument was erected as a reminder of the conflagration. On top of the memorial is a brass urn of flames. The column's height of 202 feet is significant, representing the distance from the source of the fire, a baker's shop in nearby Pudding Lane. Pudding refers not to baked goods, but to animal entrails. Butchers in Eastcheap used the lane to carry pudding to the river for disposal.

Jumping from the top of Monument was a popular method of suicide until railings were installed in 1842.

Location:	King William St, London Bridge EC4. East side of the street
Map Grid:	3b
Tube station:	Monument
Bus route:	15, 17, 25, 48, 133, 344
Architect:	John Burnet and Thomas Tait. Statue by Reid Dick
Built:	1921–25
Style:	Classical influences
Cryptic clue:	A South Australian city on London Bridge?

Adelaide House, King William Street, London Bridge EC4

Queen Adelaide may have been glad that the new London Bridge she and husband King William IV opened in 1830 was used for traffic only. A previous London Bridge had been the last destination for traitors and rebels, but only their heads. After execution, the heads were boiled and stuck on stakes above the bridge gatehouse to rot in the elements. This grisly practice was the final insult for Sir Thomas More and Scottish patriot William Wallace.

When it was built, the owners of Adelaide House proudly advertised it as having toilets on each floor, central heating and full electric lighting throughout. Such services were innovative in the early 1920s. On the roof, a garden and 18-hole putting green was used by employees. Bees were imported to fertilize the fruit trees and birds flocked to the garden in the sky.

Location:	King William St, London Bridge, EC4. West side of the street
Map Grid:	3a
Tube station:	Monument
Bus route:	5, 17, 25, 48, 133, 344
Architect:	Henry Roberts
Built:	1831–5
Style:	Greek revival
Cryptic clue:	Something's fishy

Address

Fishmongers' Hall, King William Street, London Bridge, EC4

Good Christians did not eat meat on Fridays, fasting for the sake of spiritual discipline. Fish was the alternative. The demand for fish led to great wealth and importance for the Fishmongers' Guild. Guilds were medieval trade associations with responsibilities that varied from quality control to price setting.

The Fishmongers' Guild traces its existence to the 12th century. Inside the Hall an extensive collection of art and artefacts bequeathed by Guild members is displayed. One of the artefacts is the dagger owned by William Walworth, reputedly used to stab Wat Tyler, leader of the Peasants Revolt. This is explained in more detail on page 28.

Location:	Threadneedle St., EC3. South side of the street
Map Grid:	2a
Tube station:	Bank
Bus route:	8, 11, 23, 25, 76, 133, 242
Architect:	William Tite
Built:	1841–44
Style:	Classical, with Baroque features
Cryptic clue:	Swapping goods in a regal manner

Royal Exchange, Threadneedle Street and Cornhill, EC3

Rain or shine the merchants of London conducted their business walking up and down Lombard Street. That was until the Exchange was built. Queen Elizabeth I bestowed the Royal epithet at the grand opening in 1571. It quickly became England's centre of international trade and its loss in the Great Fire of London left merchants tramping the pavements once again.

Another great Queen, Victoria, declared the current building open. It is the third Exchange on the site. The central figure in the frieze above the entrance represents Lady Commerce. Statues decorating the building include one of 14th century Lord Mayor, Richard Whittington, better known as Dick. Londoners benefited from his generous financial bequest that paid for improvements to the city water supply, and the construction of a public lavatory known as 'Whittington's Longhouse'.

Location:	Lothbury, EC2. South side of the street
Map Grid:	2a
Tube station:	Bank
Bus route:	8, 11, 23, 25, 76,133, 242
Architect:	Herbert Baker from John Soane's 18th century design
Remodelled:	1921–37
Style:	Classical
Cryptic clue:	I promise to pay the bearer on demand the sum of . . .

Bank of England, Threadneedle Street, EC2

'The Old Lady of Threadneedle Street' is the nickname of Britain's central bank. An anonymous letter sent to the Bank's directors in 1836, was cause for alarm because the writer claimed to have access to the underground bullion vault. The writer offered to meet the directors there to prove his claim. On the appointed night, they watched as the mysterious letter writer clambered up into the room through the floorboards. He was a sewer worker who a few weeks earlier had discovered a drain running under the bank. Nothing had been stolen and for his honesty he was rewarded with £800 – a significant sum in the 19th century.

The name Threadneedle is thought to relate to the Merchant Taylor's Guild that meets at number 30 Threadneedle Street.

Cryptic clue explanation: The phrase, ' I promise to pay the bearer on demand the sum of . . .' is printed on all British bank notes.

Location:	Moorgate, EC2. East side of the street
Map Grid:	1a
Tube station:	Moorgate
Bus route:	76, 214
Architect:	John Belcher and John J.Joass
Built:	1900–3
Style:	Edwardian Baroque
Cryptic clue:	Mourning becomes this woman's home

Address

London Metropolitan University, Electra House, 84 Moorgate, EC2

Moor Gate led to a marshy area called Moorfields. It was outside the city wall and the Romans used it for burials. In medieval times the marsh was drained and used for recreation, becoming a notorious locale for prostitution and crime. On a fine day, a person walking through Moorfields would likely have come across dozens of women sitting by their clean washing that was laid on the ground to dry. After the Moor Gate was demolished in the 1760s, development encroached onto Moorfields and the washer women had to find an alternative place to dry their wet clothes.

Electra House was originally the headquarters of the Eastern Telegraph Company. The cherubs in the photograph appear to be holding telegraph wires that circumnavigate the earth.

Cryptic clue explanation: 'Mourning Becomes Electra' is the title of a play by Eugene O'Neill.

Smithfield & Blackfriars

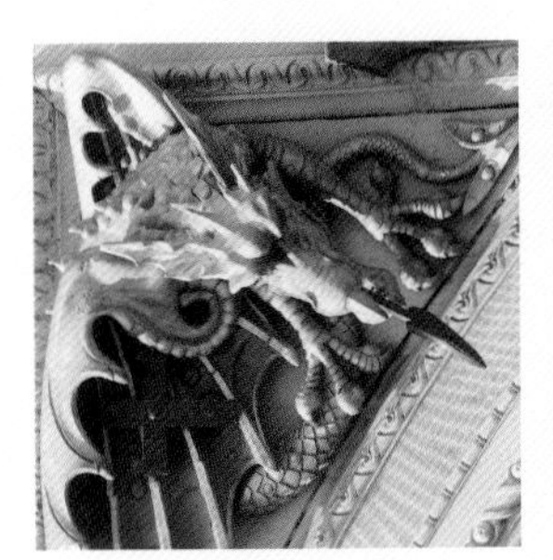

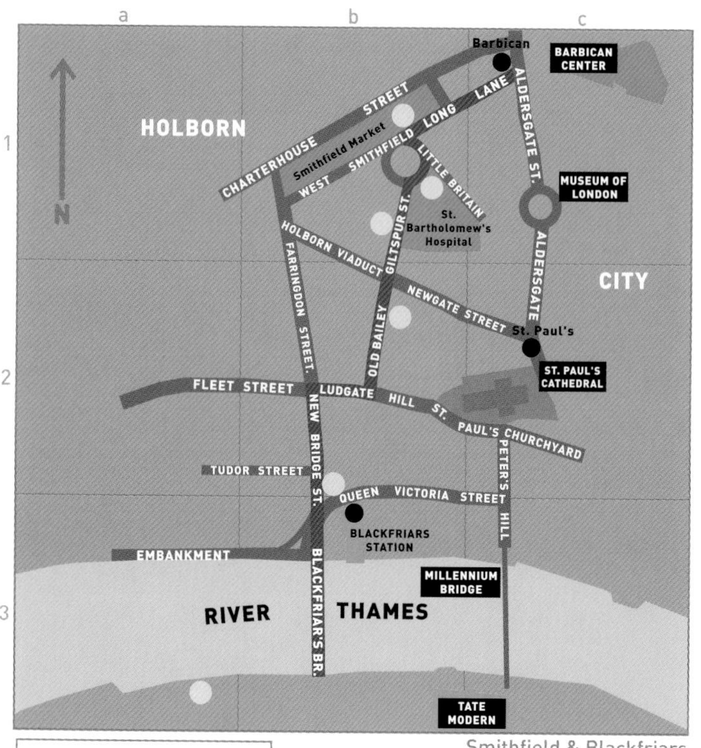

Smithfield & Blackfriars

WALKING ROUTE

MAJOR STREETS

LOCATION OF PHOTOGRAPH

LONDON UNDERGROUND STATION

MAJOR LANDMARK

PARKS & OPEN SPACES

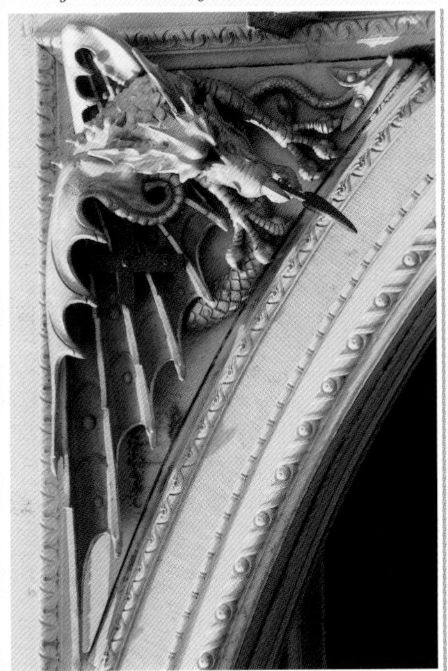

Location:	West Smithfield, EC1. West side of the street
Map grid:	1b
Tube station:	Barbican
Bus route:	4, 11, 15, 17, 23, 45, 63, 76, 100
Architect:	Horace Jones
Built:	1866–7
Style:	Cast iron industrial architecture
Cryptic clue:	Metal worker in open land

Address

Smithfield Market, Farringdon Road, EC1

If the dragon in the photograph appears to be licking his lips it is no surprise, for Smithfield is Britain's largest meat market. Smithfield has an ancient tradition of livestock trading. William Fitzstephen described Smithfield in 1174: 'a smooth field where every Friday there is a celebrated rendezvous of fine horses to be sold, and in another quarter are placed vendibles of the peasant, swine with their deep flanks, and cows and oxen of immense bulk.'

For centuries, animals were herded to market from the outlying countryside causing havoc as they trampled through the streets of London. Herding to Smithfield was discontinued in 1855 and owners of china shops in the neighbourhood no longer had to worry about bulls straying onto their premises. Today the market deals only in butchered meat.

The name Smithfield is a corruption of 'smooth field' and through the centuries it has been the location of jousts, duels and Bartholomew's Fair, an annual fourteen-day revellry of drinking, dancing and gambling.

Location:	West Smithfield, EC1. East side of the street
Map grid:	1b
Tube station:	Barbican
Bus route:	4, 11, 15, 17, 23, 45, 63, 76, 100
Architects:	Edward Strong Junior and Philip Hardwick
Built:	1702 and reconstructed in 1883–4
Style:	Baroque
Cryptic clue:	Entryway to Bart's infirmary

St Bartholomew's Hospital Gatehouse, West Smithfield, EC1

St Bart's, as the hospital is commonly known has served London since 1123. King Henry VIII threatened its existence in 1536, however, when he dissolved the adjoining priory and pocketed its revenues. Powerful businessmen lobbied the King to permit St Bart's to continue and he acquiesced, taking credit for re-founding the hospital. This explains the statue of Henry in the photograph. The reclining figures above him represent Lameness and Disease.

Blood in the streets of Smithfield did not just come from the meat market. Witches and heretics were burned to death on bonfires outside the nearby St Bartholomew-the-Great church gate.

Wat Tyler, leader of the Peasants Revolt of 1381, an uprising against unfair taxes, met his death outside the gates of St Bart's. During a meeting with the 14-year old King Richard II to discuss the peasants' grievances, an altercation ensued. Tyler was stabbed in the neck by William Walworth, the Lord Mayor. The injured peasant took refuge in the hospital but was dragged out by the King's forces and beheaded.

Location:	Giltspur St., EC1. West side of the street
Map grid:	1b
Tube station:	Barbican
Bus route:	4, 11, 15, 17, 23, 45, 63, 76, 100
Sculptor.	Unknown
Built:	17th century
Cryptic clue:	It's a Bart's and Bailey world

City and Guilds, 1 Giltspur Street, EC1

This is the Golden Boy of Pye Corner and he represents the sin of gluttony, or so the unknown Londoner who commissioned the sculpture believed. The Golden Boy is on the site of a pub, 'The Fortune of War', demolished in the late 19th century. Here, surgeons from St Bart's Hospital shopped for newly executed corpses for use in dissection class by medical students. The cadavers, former inmates of Newgate Jail, were stolen from a nearby church cemetery by grave robbers known as 'Resurrection Men'.

Cock Lane, which runs by the side of the Golden Boy was infamous for prostitution, male and female, and was the only site in London where it was legal. The colourful street name must have left passers-by in no doubt about the thoroughfare's commerce.

Giltspur Street was known in the 16th century as Gyltspurstreate meaning 'the street where gilt spurs were made.' Knights competing in tournaments at the adjacent Smithfield could shop for spurs before jousts.

Cryptic clue explanation: The Golden Boy is situated between St Bart's Hospital and Old Bailey. The clue is a play on the lyric 'It's a Barnum and Bailey World' from the song 'Paper Moon'.

Location:	Old Bailey, EC1. East side of the street
Map grid:	2b
Tube station:	Blackfriars or St Paul's
Bus route:	4, 11, 15, 17, 23, 45, 63, 76, 100
Architect:	Edward Mountford. Statues by Frederick William Pomeroy
Built:	1900–7
Style:	Edwardian Baroque
Cryptic clue:	Justice is blind

Central Criminal Court, Old Bailey, EC1

Newgate Prison was so infernal that many of the inmates died before their sentence was served. Death came at the hands of brutal prisoners and even more savage guards or by disease that flourished in the poorly ventilated hellhole. From the 12th century it stood on the site now occupied by the Central Criminal Court. Newgate Prison housed a variety of criminals: – from debtors to heretics, thieves to murderers. Two of English literature's great writers, Daniel Defoe and Oscar Wilde, were incarcerated in Newgate Prison.

Next door to Newgate was a sessions house where judges dispensed justice. The stench from the prison was so vile that court officials carried posies of flowers to sweeten the air. They also believed the flowers would ward off 'jail fever' (typhoid). Today, court officials still carry flowers at the beginning of law sessions but for the sake of tradition only.

The name 'Old Bailey' was recorded in 1311 as Le Baille, from the Middle English word *baille* meaning 'defensive rampart on the outside of the City wall'.

The statues in the photograph represent Truth, Fortitude and the Recording Angel.

Cryptic clue explanation: A statue of Justice, blindfold, stands on top of the Central Criminal Court.

Location:	Queen Victoria St, EC4. East side of the street
Map Grid:	2b
Tube station:	Blackfriars
Bus route:	4, 11, 15, 17, 23, 45, 63, 76, 100
Architect:	H. Fuller-Clark
Built:	1875
Style:	Arts and Crafts
Cryptic clue:	Religious men in black imbibe here

Black Friar, 174 Queen Victoria Street, EC4

The Black Friar public house was named after the 13th century Dominican monastery formerly on the site. The friars wore black robes. When King Henry VIII dissolved the monastery in 1536 the buildings were given to a royal courtier with the job title, Keeper of the Royal Tents and Master of the Revels.

Bridewell Palace formerly stood on a site opposite the pub. It was used as a jail in the 16th century. Public floggings were dispensed outside the gates, and a ducking stool punished prisoners by submerging them in the Thames, sometimes for minutes at a time.

The ground floor bars in the Black Friar were decorated with marble, bronze and mosaics circa 1904. In the 1960s, the site was marked for demolition but a public outcry succeeded in saving London's only remaining Arts and Crafts building. The pub is closed at weekends.

Location:	Barge House St., SE1. (View it from Blackfriars Bridge). South bank of the river
Map Grid:	3a
Tube station:	Blackfriars
Bus route:	4, 11, 15, 17, 23, 45, 63, 76, 100
Architect:	A.W. Moore
Built:	1928
Style:	Art Deco
Cryptic clue:	This building's product was always in stock

Oxo Tower, Barge House Street, SE1

OXO, incorporated into the structure of the tower using glazed lights, was a cheeky manoeuvre around a law that forbade buildings from carrying advertising signs. London County Council was not amused when the tower, with its indiscreet signage, visible for miles, was erected. A demand for demolition was issued but not enforced.

The building was formerly the Oxo Warehouse (Oxo is the trade name of a stock cube), but was disused by the 1970s. Redevelopment plans for the surrounding area called for the building's demolition but a public campaign succeeded in saving the warehouse. Today it is apartments, with the top floor used as a restaurant.

King James I berthed his Royal Barge in a boathouse on this site in the 17th century.

Fleet Street, Strand & Aldwych

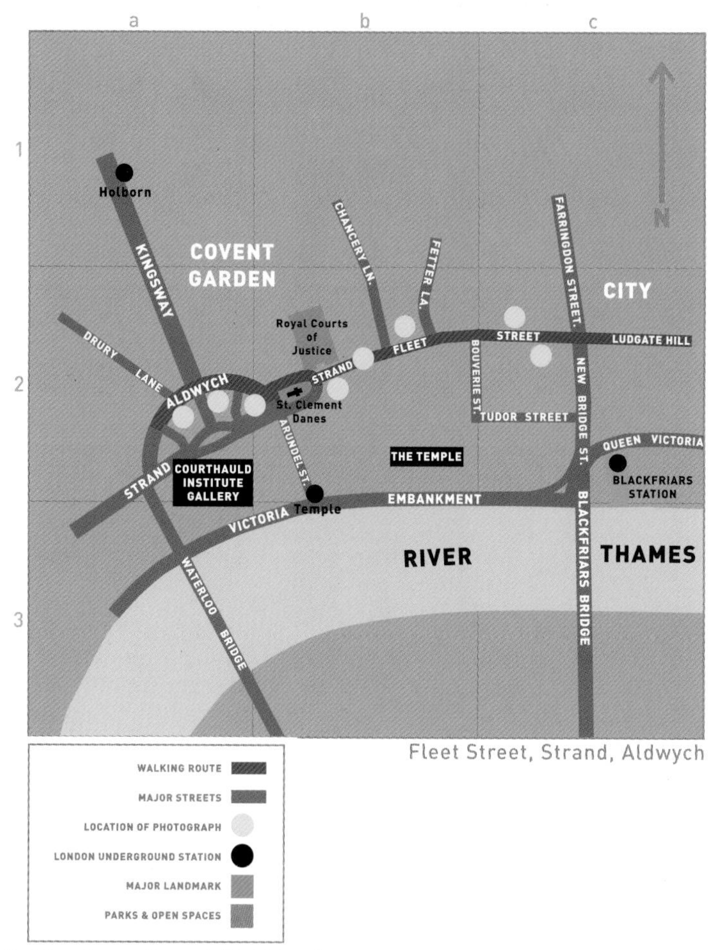

Fleet Street, Strand, Aldwych

Location:	Fleet Street, EC4. South side of the street
Map grid:	2c
Tube station:	Blackfriars
Bus route:	4, 11, 15, 17, 23, 45, 63, 76, 100
Architect:	Christopher Wren
Built:	1670–84
Style:	Baroque
Cryptic clue:	Always the bridesmaid, never the ??? beatified

St Bride Church, Fleet Street, EC4

St Bride's spire is often cited as the most beautiful in London. Until 1764 when it was struck by lightning, the spire was eight feet taller. A parishioner working as a confectioner was so inspired by the spire he created cakes in tiers, setting the pattern for wedding cakes to this day.

St Bride was built on the site of a 6th century Saxon church, London's earliest Christian place of worship. Wartime bombing in 1940 badly damaged the church, and during renovations, the remains of a Roman house were discovered in the crypt. These and other artefacts in the crypt museum tell the story of the church. Among the exhibits is a lockable coffin from the 18th century when body snatching was rife.

Location:	Fleet St, EC4. North side of the street
Map grid:	2c
Tube station:	Blackfriars
Bus route:	4, 11, 15, 17, 23, 45, 63, 76, 100
Architects:	Elcock & Sutcliffe with Thomas Tait. Clock by the Birmingham Guild
Built:	1928–31
Style:	Art Deco
Cryptic clue:	Street of the collective noun of ships, 135 times over

135–141 Fleet Street, EC4

Fleet Street is named after the Fleet River that now runs underground below Farringdon Street. In the 16th century, Fleet Street became London's centre of publishing when a printer named Wynkyn de Worde opened an office to serve the printing needs of lawyers based at Temple Inn.

For years Fleet Street has been a euphemism for the national newspaper industry although there are no longer any newspapers published on the street. The building in the photograph was formerly the headquarters of the Daily Telegraph. The black glass building next door previously housed the Daily Express and its streamlined facade is a good example of Art Deco architecture.

Location:	Fleet St, EC4. North side of the street
Map Grid:	2b
Tube station:	Temple (closed on Sundays)
Bus route:	4, 11, 15, 17, 23, 45, 63, 76, 100
Architect:	John Shaw. Clock by Thomas Harris in 1671
Built:	1831–3
Style:	Gothic revival
Cryptic clue:	Saintly patron of goldsmiths, where the sun goes down

St Dunstan in the West, Fleet Street, EC4

St Dunstan is the patron saint of goldsmiths, jewellers and locksmiths and he has two city churches named after him. The current church was built on the site of a medieval church of the same name. Grateful parishioners commissioned the clock in thanks to God for sparing St Dunstan's from the flames of the Great Fire of London. The clock dates from 1671. On the hour, models of the mythical giants Gog and Magog, traditional guardians of the city, strike the bells with their clubs.

The figure of Elizabeth I on the church wall to the right of the clock is the only surviving statue of the Queen sculpted in her lifetime (1586). It originally stood on Ludgate, a city gate now demolished.

Location: Fleet St, EC4. Middle of the street
Map grid: 2b
Nearest tube: Temple (closed on Sundays)
Bus route: 4, 11, 15, 17, 23, 45, 63, 76, 100
Architect: Horace Jones
Built: 1880
Style: Victorian
Cryptic clue: A religious hostelry

Temple Bar, Fleet Street, EC4

Temple Bar marks the western boundary of the City of London. A gate stood on this site for centuries. Since Elizabethan times, to this day, when the Monarch enters the City, an ancient ceremony is conducted at Temple Bar. He or she is met at the Bar by the Lord Mayor and asks permission to proceed. The City was for hundreds of years a self-governing entity and the Lord Mayor was the pre-eminent citizen. The Lord Mayor hands a ceremonial sword to the Monarch, symbolically relinquishing precedence and permits entry. The sword is handed back so the Lord Mayor can protect the Monarch while they are in the City precincts.

The bronze relief on the current structure represents Queen Victoria's visits to the City.

Location:	Strand, WC2. South side of the street
Map grid:	2b
Tube station:	Temple (closed on Sundays)
Bus route:	4, 6, 9, 11, 13, 15, 23, 59, 68, 76, 77a, 91, 168, 188, 341
Architect:	Unknown
Statues built:	1787
Style:	Georgian
Cryptic clue:	All the tea in China

Twinings Tea, 216, Strand, WC2

Street numbers did not exist when Thomas Twining established his tea business in 1706, so the Golden Lion logo identified his company. In the 18th century, all tea came from China, hence the nationality of the men in the photograph.

Until 1784, the British government tax on tea was so prohibitive that smuggling was rife. Richard Twining, grandson of the founder, persuaded Prime Minister William Pitt to reduce the duty. Imports of tea doubled, smuggling ceased and it became available to most people, making tea Britain's national drink.

Twinings is one of few businesses in London still trading from its original premises and is run by the same family that founded it.

The Chinese figures and Golden Lion are made of Coade stone. Coade stone is an artificial stone named after Mrs Eleanor Coade. Her secret recipe was a mixture of clay, sand and glass, with a hard surface finish fired in a kiln. It was used in building construction during the 18th and early 19th century.

Location:	Aldwych and Strand, WC2. Corner of the street
Map grid:	2b
Tube station:	Temple (closed on Sundays)
Bus route:	4, 6, 9, 11, 13, 15, 23, 59, 68, 76, 77a, 91, 168, 188, 341
Architect:	A.M. MacKenzie and A.G.R. MacKenzie. Statues by Bertram MacKennal
Built:	1912–18
Style:	Romanesque
Cryptic clue:	Antipodean dwelling

Australia House, Strand, WC2

Helios and the Horses of the Sun sculpted in bronze stand proudly surveying Strand from the top of Australia's High Commission.

On the traffic island opposite Australia House is the church of St Clement Danes. Christopher Wren designed the current church in the 17th century but there has been a church on the site for hundreds of years. Its association with Danes is unclear. Danish forces invaded London in the Dark Ages and it is suggested that notable Danes were buried at the church.

The word 'strand' comes from the old English word *stronde*, meaning 'bank' or 'shore'. This street was recorded as Strand in 1185 when it was adjacent to the Thames. Since the Victoria Embankment was built in the 19th century, Strand no longer looks onto the river.

Location:	Aldwych, WC2. South side of the street
Map grid:	2a
Nearest tube:	Holborn or Temple (closed on Sundays)
Bus route:	4, 6, 9, 11, 13, 15, 23, 59, 68, 76, 77a, 91, 168, 188, 341
Architects:	Helmle & Corbett. Statues by Malvina Hoffman
Built:	1925–35
Style:	Classical
Cryptic clue:	A service to the world of radio

Bush House, Aldwych, WC2

'Youth', as the statues in the photograph are known, represents the enduring friendship between England and America. Bush House, named for the American businessman who commissioned the building, has been the headquarters of the British Broadcasting Corporation's World Service since 1940.

An ambitious redevelopment programme at the beginning of the 20th century swept away acres of notorious slums that blighted this corner of London. Charles Dickens wrote of them in his novel 'Bleak House'. Ignoring the previous pattern of narrow and haphazard streets, town-planners designed the gracious crescent of Aldwych, and the wide boulevard of Kingsway in a design that owes more to Paris in its appearance than to London.

Location:	Aldwych, WC2. South side of the street
Map grid:	2a
Tube station:	Holborn or Temple (closed on Sundays)
Bus route:	4, 6, 9, 11, 13, 15, 23, 59, 68, 76, 77a, 91, 168, 188, 341
Architects:	Herbert Baker and A.T. Scott
Built:	1928–30
Style:	Classical
Cryptic clue:	A subcontinent's high commission

India House, Aldwych, WC2

Several emblems adorn the exterior of India House, each one representing an Indian province. The Fort of St George in the photograph depicts Madras. Other symbols include a rhinoceros for Assam and a peacock representing Burma. At the time India House was built, Burma was part of British India. During the ceremony to open India House, King George V used a solid gold key to unlock the main gates.

Inside the High Commission, magnificent murals showcase the talents of four Indian artists chosen in a competition to decorate India's London embassy. For the artists it was a unique opportunity. They visited European cities to learn the technique of painting on plaster and were tutored at London's Royal College of Art before creating the colourful visual works based on Indian legends.

Trafalgar Square & Leicester Square

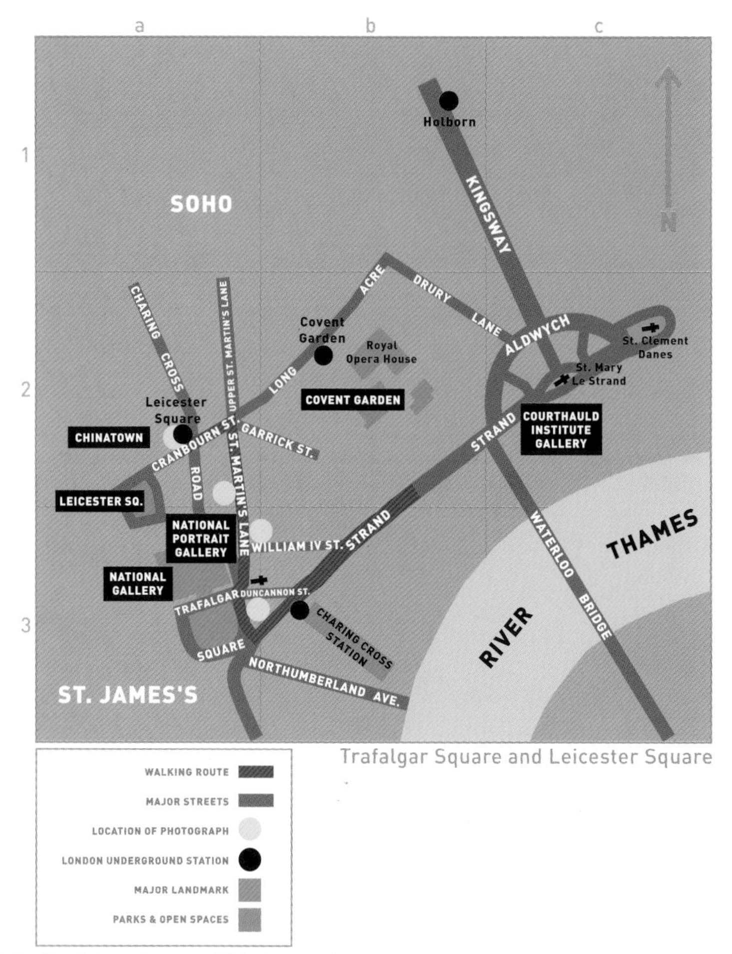

Trafalgar Square and Leicester Square

Location:	Trafalgar Square, SW1. East side of the square
Map grid:	3a
Tube station:	Charing Cross and Embankment
Bus route:	3, 6, 9, 11, 12, 13, 15, 23, 24, 53, 77a, 88, 91, 139, 159
Architect:	Herbert Baker. Sculpture by Charles Wheeler
Built:	1935–7
Style:	Classical
Cryptic clue:	Two Nelsons, one on the column, one in the High Commission

Address

South Africa House, Trafalgar Square, SW1

Trafalgar Square is named after a naval battle fought off the coast of Spain in 1805. British forces led by Admiral Lord Nelson were victorious. Nelson is honoured by the column in the Square upon which his statue stands.

Trafalgar Square is the symbolic heart of London.
Its proximity to the Houses of Parliament and government buildings in Whitehall has made the square a favoured location for political demonstrations. But it also draws less serious crowds. Traditionally on New Year's Eve, tens of thousands of revellers gather in Trafalgar Square to hear Big Ben chime midnight.

An empty plinth in the square has attracted many suggestions about who is worthy enough to merit a statue on such hallowed ground. During the 2002 Soccer World Cup, that honour temporarily went to David Beckham, the England team captain, when his waxen image from Madame Tussaud's Waxworks was stealthily placed upon the plinth.

The golden gazelle in the photograph is a Springbok, South Africa's national animal.

Location:	St Martin's Lane, WC2. East side of the street
Map grid:	3a
Tube station:	Leicester Square and Charing Cross
Bus route:	3, 6, 9, 11, 12, 13, 15, 23, 24, 53, 77a, 88, 91, 139, 159
Automaton builder:	Unknown
Built:	1970s
Cryptic clue:	Portrait of a Cooper

Chandos Pub, 29 St Martin's Lane, WC2

What is the Cooper in the photograph hammering? A Firkin or a Kilderkin? Those are the names of wooden beer barrels. Coopers are practitioners of a dying craft. They make wooden beer barrels in an industry where most beer is stored in metal containers. Brewing giant Samuel Smith, the owner of The Chandos still employs a cooper for the wooden casks containing its Brewery Bitter.

Covent Garden (where The Chandos is situated), is a corruption of the medieval 'convent garden' of Westminster Abbey. After the Dissolution of the Monasteries by King Henry VIII, the convent garden was bestowed on the Russell family, supporters of the King. Covent Garden was the place to live in the 17th century when architect Inigo Jones created the first square in London, the Piazza. Wealthy residents were peeved when a fruit, vegetable and flower market flourished in the Piazza. They moved to more desirable neighbourhoods and the area fell from fashion.

Eliza Doolittle, George Bernard Shaw's character in the play *Pygmalion* sold flowers at Covent Garden market.

Cryptic clue explanation: The Chandos is opposite the National Portrait Gallery.

Location:	St Martins Lane, WC2. West side of the street
Map grid:	2a
Tube station:	Leicester Square and Charing Cross
Bus route:	3, 6, 9, 11, 12, 13, 15, 23, 24, 53, 77a, 88, 91, 139, 159
Architect:	Unknown
Built:	1890s
Style:	Classical features
Cryptic clue:	Two of four, the others next door, where you can come on into the palace of gin.

Zippi Restaurant, 92 St Martins Lane, WC2

Cherubim are considered by Christians to sit in the very presence of God and traditionally the colour surrounding them is blue. Not so the cherubim in this photograph or their gold and black twins above the door of the adjacent Salisbury pub.

Little is known about the history of the building in the photograph. It is thought to have been a restaurant when it was built and if so it was well placed because late 19th century St Martin's Lane was a burgeoning entertainment spot with several theatres and public houses.

The Salisbury has a spectacular interior, rich with ornate carving and mirrors. It is one of London's few remaining Victorian gin palaces.

Location:	Cranbourn Street, WC2. North side of the street
Map grid:	2a
Tube station:	Leicester Square
Bus route:	24, 29, 176
Architect:	Frank Matcham
Built:	1899–1900
Style:	French Renaissance
Cryptic clue:	A place where the African river horse races

Hippodrome, Charing Cross Road, WC2

Polar bears in Leicester Square? In 1909, thanks to the Hippodrome music hall, customers had the chance to witness a water spectacle called 'The Arctic' that featured dozens of polar bears in a giant water tank. Water was piped in from a stream called 'Cran bourn' that runs under the building. Although the audience may not have been safe from splashes, they were protected from the bears by a 12 foot high fence surrounding the pool.

Leicester Square was laid out in the 1670s and was surrounded by the grand houses of the aristocracy. Until the Dissolution of the Monasteries, Westminster Abbey owned this area of London and it was common land where parishioners were permitted to graze their animals and dry their washing.

After the construction of Coventry Street circa 1750, Leicester Square residents moved out as increased traffic destroyed the quiet atmosphere. Shops, hotels, and later theatres and Turkish baths, moved in, attracting revellers, who were predominantly male. Leicester Square became a place where no self-respecting unescorted lady was seen.

Holborn & Bloomsbury

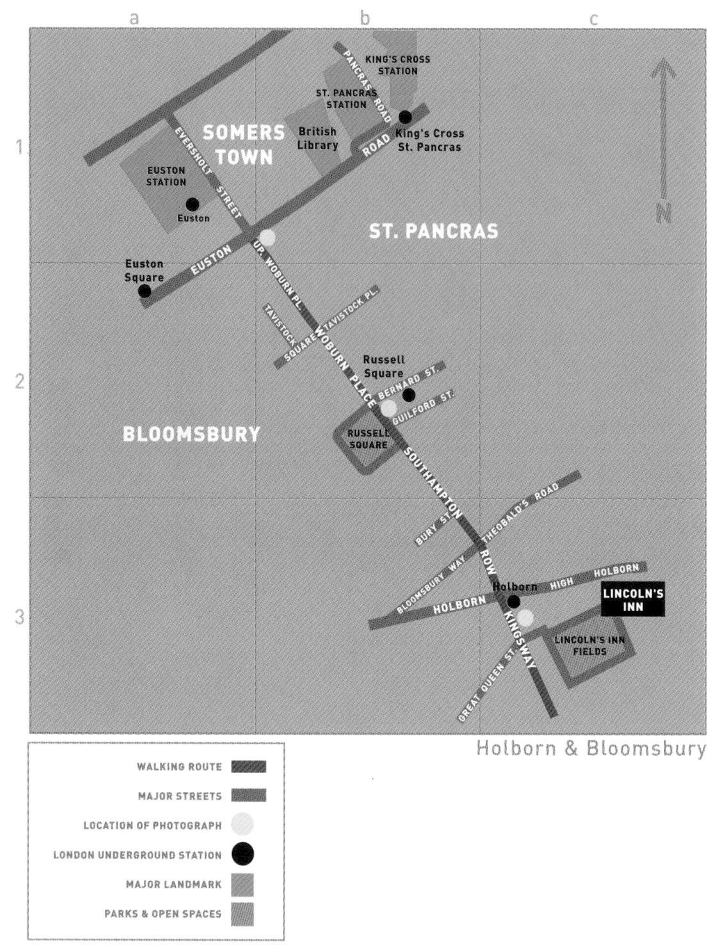
a
b
c
1
2
3
KING'S CROSS STATION
PANCRAS ROAD
ST. PANCRAS STATION
SOMERS TOWN
British Library
ROAD
King's Cross St. Pancras
EVERSHOLT STREET
EUSTON STATION
Euston
ST. PANCRAS
Euston Square
EUSTON
UP. WOBURN PL.
TAVISTOCK PL.
TAVISTOCK SQUARE
WOBURN PLACE
Russell Square
BERNARD ST.
GUILFORD ST.
BLOOMSBURY
RUSSELL SQUARE
SOUTHAMPTON ROW
THEOBALD'S ROAD
BURY ST.
BLOOMSBURY WAY
Holborn
HIGH HOLBORN
HOLBORN
LINCOLN'S INN
KINGSWAY
LINCOLN'S INN FIELDS
GREAT QUEEN ST.
N
Holborn & Bloomsbury
WALKING ROUTE
MAJOR STREETS
LOCATION OF PHOTOGRAPH
LONDON UNDERGROUND STATION
MAJOR LANDMARK
PARKS & OPEN SPACES

Location:	Kingsway, WC2. East side of the street
Map grid:	3c
Tube station:	Holborn
Bus route:	8, 19, 25, 38, 55, 59, 68, 91, 98, 168, 188, 242
Architects:	Trehearne & Norman. Sculptor: Benjamin Clemens
Built:	1921
Style:	A mixture of Doric Order and Florentine palazzo
Cryptic clue:	A Dark Continent dwelling on the route of the male monarch

Africa House, 64–78 Kingsway, WC2

The group of statues on the facade of Africa House formed a subtle advertisement for the building's first tenant, the African and Eastern Trade Corporation.

Kingsway was laid out at the beginning of the 20th century and it replaced extensive slums that stretched through Covent Garden to Oxford Street. Overcrowded tenement buildings known as 'rookeries' bred disease, misery and crime. They were filthy, damp and rat infested. Looking at Kingsway and Covent Garden today it is hard to imagine that just over a century ago, the area was among the most poverty-stricken in London.

Location: Russell Square, WC1. East side of the street
Map grid: 2b
Tube station: Russell Square
Bus route: 7, 59, 68, 91, 168, 188
Architect: Charles Fitzroy Doll
Built: 1898
Style: French Chateau
Cryptic clue: Accommodation in canine Jack's square

Hotel Russell, Russell Square, WC1

When the Hotel Russell was completed, it was not only the first Victorian structure in Bloomsbury, but it was twice as high as its neighbours. The Hotel Russell was unique in the overwhelmingly Georgian architecture of Bloomsbury, not least because of the acres of terracotta on its facade.

Charles Fitzroy Doll based his designs for the hotel on the Chateau de Madrid, that stood in Paris's Bois de Boulogne in the 16th century.

Bloomsbury was first mentioned in 1242 as *Soca Blemund,* meaning, 'district under the jurisdiction of Blemund'. It was later referred to as *Blomsburye* a Middle English word that meant 'manor held by the de Blemund family'.

Location:	Upper Woburn Place, WC1. East side of the street
Map grid:	1b
Nearest tube:	Euston
Bus route:	10, 18, 30, 59, 68, 73, 91, 168
Architects:	Henry & William Inwood. Caryatids created by J.F.C. Rossi
Built:	1819–22
Style:	Greek revival
Cryptic clue:	Sounds like the church of a saintly human organ

St Pancras Church, Upper Woburn Place, WC1

Pancratius is not a disease, it is the name of a 14-year old Roman Christian convert who, according to legend, was martyred in the fourth century by Emperor Diocletian. Pancratius has two London churches named after him. This St Pancras Church is not to be confused with Old St Pancras Church, north of King's Cross where Saxon remains dating from AD600 identify the old church as one of the earliest Christian sites in Europe.

St Pancras Church was the first Greek Revival church in London. The design was inspired by the Temple of Erechtheum at the Acropolis in Athens. An original caryatid from the Temple of Erechtheum can be viewed in the British Museum and forms part of a collection of Ancient Greek marble treasures known as the Elgin Marbles.

Oxford Circus

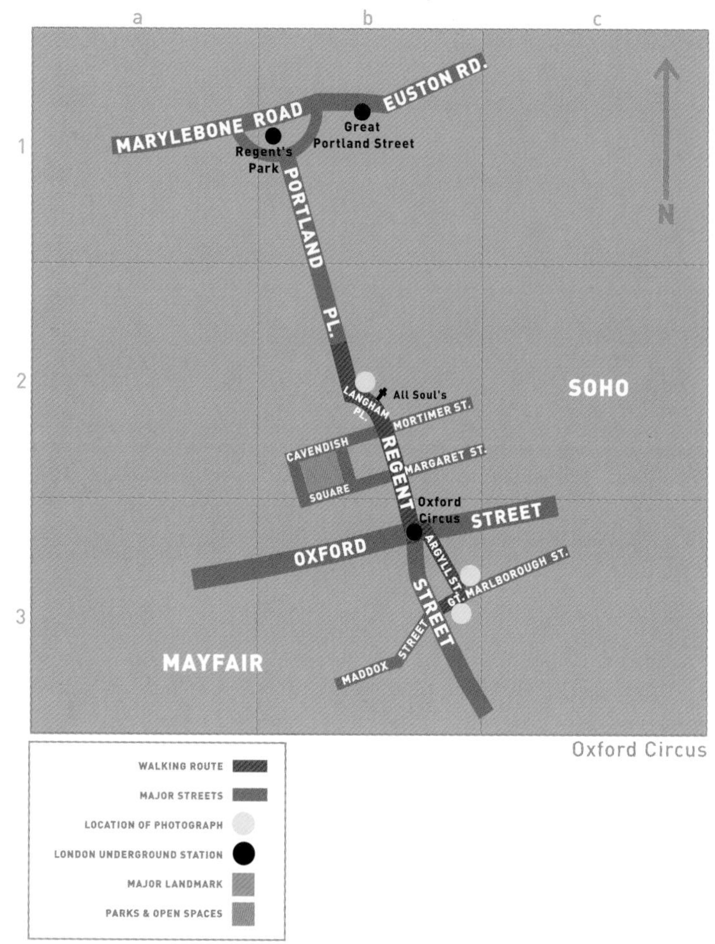
a
b
c
1
2
3
N
MARYLEBONE ROAD
EUSTON RD.
Regent's Park
Great Portland Street
PORTLAND
PL.
All Soul's
LANGHAM PL.
MORTIMER ST.
CAVENDISH
SQUARE
REGENT
MARGARET ST.
Oxford Circus
STREET
OXFORD
ARGYLL ST.
GT. MARLBOROUGH ST.
STREET
MADDOX STREET
SOHO
MAYFAIR
Oxford Circus
WALKING ROUTE
MAJOR STREETS
LOCATION OF PHOTOGRAPH
LONDON UNDERGROUND STATION
MAJOR LANDMARK
PARKS & OPEN SPACES

Location:	Langham Place, W1. East side of the street
Map grid:	2b
Tube station:	Oxford Circus
Bus route:	3, 6, 7, 8, 10, 12, 13, 15, 23, 25, 53, 55, 73, 88, 94, 98, 137, 139, 159, C2
Architect:	Val Myers and Watson-Hart. Sculptures by Eric Gill
Built:	1931
Style:	Art Deco
Cryptic clue:	Broadcasting on the waves north of the circus

BBC Broadcasting House, Langham Place, W1

Prospero and Ariel, characters from Shakespeare's *The Tempest,* stand above the door of BBC Broadcasting House. Ariel, the invisible spirit of the air is to be sent out into the world by his master Prospero.

The clock on the building's facade is silent, so the BBC imports bell chimes to announce certain news programmes. As Big Ben strikes the hour in the clock tower of the Houses of Parliament, a microphone relays the chimes to Broadcasting House for live transmission.

Cryptic clue explanation: Broadcasting House is the home of BBC Radio and is located north of Oxford Circus.

Location:	Argyll St, W1. East side of the street
Map grid:	3b
Tube station:	Oxford Street
Bus route:	3, 6, 7, 8, 10, 12, 13, 15, 23, 25, 53, 55, 73, 88, 94, 98, 137, 139, 159, C2
Architects:	Raymond Hood and G. Jeeves
Built:	1928
Style:	Art Deco
Cryptic clue:	House of the white ductile metallic element

Palladium House, 1–4 Argyll Street, W1

Art Deco golden flames adorn the upper part of Palladium House, a visual reference to its first tenant, a heating company. When Palladium House was built, Art Deco was very stylish. Black marble was chosen for the facade because it would not discolour in the smoggy London air.

Argyll Street takes its name from the 2nd Duke of Argyll. He was a general in the British army that defeated the ambitions of French King Louis XIV to dominate Spain in the early 18th century.

Location:	Great Marlborough St, W1. South side of the street
Map grid:	3b
Tube station:	Oxford Street
Bus route:	3, 6, 7, 8, 10, 12, 13, 15, 23, 25, 53, 55, 73, 88, 94, 98, 137, 139, 159, C2
Architects:	Edwin T. Hall and Edwin S. Hall
Built:	1924
Style:	Tudor revival
Cryptic clue:	Another word for freedom

Liberty & Co., 214 Regent Street, W1

Walk along Regent Street past all the grey Classical building facades and turn onto Great Marlborough Street to the Liberty department store. The contrast is startling. Tudor revival or 'mock-Tudor' was popular in the 1920s when Liberty & Co. was built. With its timber frame and ornate brick chimneys, Liberty resembles the buildings of London six centuries ago. Recycled timber from the decommissioned 19th century Royal Navy ships HMS *Impregnable* and HMS *Hindustan* were the source of the building materials of the Tudor wing.

Great Marlborough Street is named after the Duke of Marlborough, a military general who was victorious in the 18th century battles of the War of Spanish Succession. The Duke was an ancestor of Prime Minister Winston Churchill.

Marylebone

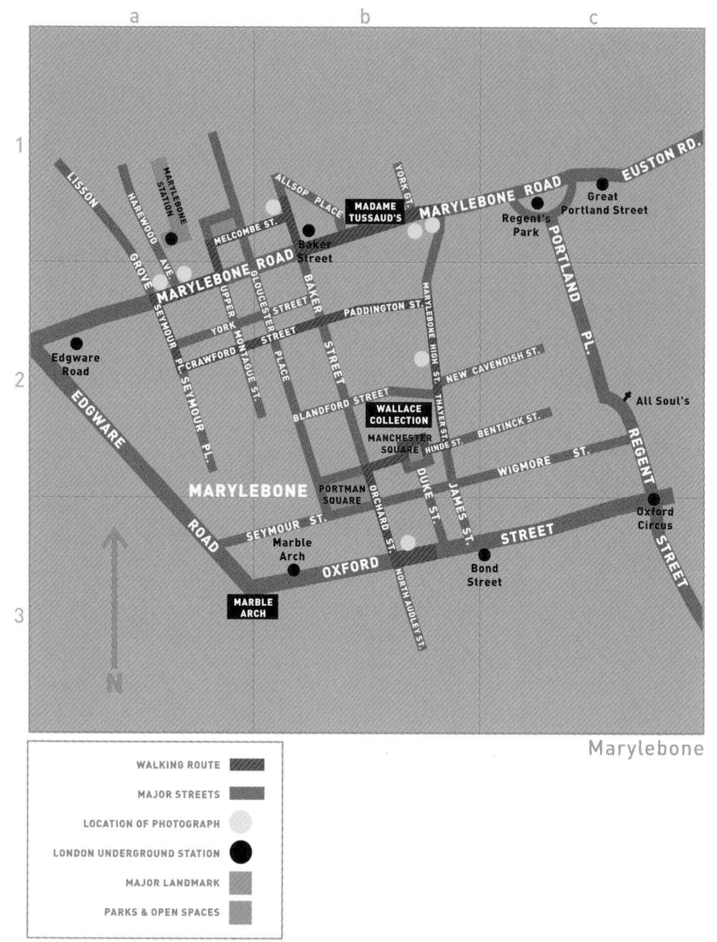
a
b
c
1
2
3
LISSON
GROVE
HAREWOOD AVE.
MARYLEBONE STATION
MELCOMBE ST.
ALLSOP PLACE
MADAME TUSSAUD'S
YORK GT.
MARYLEBONE ROAD
EUSTON RD.
Great Portland Street
Regent's Park
Baker Street
UPPER MONTAGUE ST.
GLOUCESTER PLACE
BAKER STREET
YORK STREET
PADDINGTON ST.
CRAWFORD STREET
SEYMOUR PL.
Edgware Road
EDGWARE ROAD
MARYLEBONE HIGH ST.
NEW CAVENDISH ST.
PORTLAND PL.
All Soul's
BLANDFORD STREET
WALLACE COLLECTION
THAYER ST.
MANCHESTER SQUARE
HINDE ST.
BENTINCK ST.
REGENT STREET
WIGMORE ST.
MARYLEBONE
PORTMAN SQUARE
ORCHARD ST.
DUKE ST.
JAMES ST.
Oxford Circus
SEYMOUR ST.
Marble Arch
OXFORD STREET
Bond Street
MARBLE ARCH
NORTH AUDLEY ST.
N
Marylebone
WALKING ROUTE
MAJOR STREETS
LOCATION OF PHOTOGRAPH
LONDON UNDERGROUND STATION
MAJOR LANDMARK
PARKS & OPEN SPACES

Location:	Marylebone Rd, NW1. South side of the street
Map grid:	1b
Tube station:	Baker Street
Bus route:	2, 13, 18, 27, 30, 74, 82, 139, 274
Bas-relief:	Estcourt J. Clack
Built:	1960
Cryptic clue:	A carving, not a waxwork of Mr Dickens

15 Marylebone Road, NW1

Charles Dickens wrote six of his best-known novels when he lived in a house on the site of this photograph. The bas-relief depicts characters from *David Copperfield, The Old Curiosity Shop* and *A Christmas Carol.* The bird in the bas-relief is Dickens pet raven, Grip.

Several individuals in *David Copperfield* were based on true-life residents of Marylebone.

Cryptic clue explanation: Madame Tussaud's Waxworks is on the opposite side of Marylebone Road.

Location:	Marylebone Rd, NW1. South side of the street
Map grid:	1b
Tube station:	Baker Street
Bus route:	2, 13, 18, 27, 30, 74, 82, 139, 274
Architect:	Thomas Hardwicke. Caryatids by J.F.C. Rossi
Built:	1813–17
Style:	Greek revival
Cryptic clue:	St Marylebone's faithful visit here each Sunday

St Marylebone Parish Church,
17 Marylebone Road, NW1

Charles Dickens had no distance to travel when his son was baptised at St Marylebone Parish Church. He lived next door. Dickens describes the ceremony in his novel *Dombey and Son.*

St Marylebone Church has been the scene of several noted events, from baptisms: poet Lord Byron, to weddings: philosopher Francis Bacon, and writer Elizabeth Barrett Browning. This is the third church dedicated to St Marylebone on the same site.

Location:	Baker St, NW1. West side of the street
Map grid:	1b
Tube station:	Baker Street
Bus route:	2, 13, 18, 27, 30, 74, 82, 139, 274
Architect:	John J. Joass and Daniel Warry
Built:	1932
Style:	Functionalism
Cryptic clue:	Countrywide community of monks

Abbey National, 215–229 Baker Street, NW1

Sherlock Holmes was a fictitious character but not to the thousands of people who have written to the sleuth at 221b Baker Street. That address does not exist but if it did, it would be on the premises of the Abbey National offices pictured in the photograph. At one time, the Abbey National had a member of staff dedicated to handling the correspondence that arrived for Sherlock Holmes.

Baker Street was named after William Baker, the builder who laid out the streets in this part of Marylebone in the 18th century.

Location:	Marylebone Rd, NW1. North side of the street
Map grid:	2a
Tube station:	Baker Street or Marylebone
Bus route:	2, 13, 18, 27, 30, 74, 82, 139, 274
Architect:	Robert W. Edis. Restored as a hotel by 'S' International Architects
Built:	1897–9, restored 1989–91
Style:	Renaissance
Cryptic clue:	A conspicuous object or a prominent event

Landmark London Hotel, 222 Marylebone Road, NW1

Who knows what undercover activities went on at this hotel during World War II. The Great Central Hotel as it was then known was used by MI6, the British spy agency. MI6 had a convenient camouflage because the government had requisitioned the hotel as accommodation for military personnel in transit through Marylebone Railway Station. It was the second time the Great Central had been used by the government. In World War I its role was as a convalescent home for injured soldiers. The staff canteen was employed as a morgue for the soldiers who did not recover.

Described as a 'temple of luxury' by the hotel management in its early years, the Great Central had a covered inner courtyard that allowed guests in carriages to drive right into the hotel. When cars replaced horses, this service was discontinued because of noise and petrol fumes.

Location:	Marylebone Rd, NW1. North side of the street
Map grid:	2a
Tube station:	Baker Street or Marylebone
Bus route:	2, 13, 18, 27, 30, 74, 82, 139, 274
Architect:	Richard Seifert
Built:	1955
Style:	A Mixture of Styles
Cryptic clue:	Worth its weight in wool

Woolworth House, 242 Marylebone Road, NW1

Motorists at a standstill in heavy traffic on Marylebone Road may not believe that it was Britain's first bypass. Built in 1757 and called the New Road, it was a fast route from the west into the City.

Behind the Woolworth building is an area called Lisson Grove. Nowadays it contains dozens of public housing estates and there is no hint of its rural past as an 11th century settlement named after Lilestone manor. Until development began in Marylebone in the 18th century, Lisson Grove was covered with market gardens.

Marylebone was known as Maryburne in 1453 then Marybourne, and finally Marylebone in 1626, meaning 'the place of St Mary's stream', from the old English word *burna*.

Location:	Marylebone High St, NW1
Map grid:	2b
Tube station:	Baker Street
Bus route:	2, 13, 18, 27, 30, 74, 82, 139, 274
Architect:	W.Bratford
Built:	1892
Style:	Jacobean
Cryptic clue:	Mary of the Bourne's meandering main street

109 Marylebone High Street, NW1

Re-invention of image is not a modern concept. Just look at the Marylebone Gardens that stood north of Marylebone High Street. The 17th century gardens offered bloody diversions to gamblers and thrill seekers in the form of bear and bull baiting, cock and dog-fights, and bare-fist boxing. Customers were not of the highest calibre and so, determined to improve their bad reputation, the owners of the gardens performed a makeover. An entrance charge was initiated to keep out the riffraff and the entertainment was changed to concerts, balls and pretty gardens to stroll in. It was not long before the only tarts for sale accompanied cups of tea.

Although it now features a white horse, the building in the photograph was formerly a public house called the Black Horse. It replaced a pub that had been in business since 1765 when the street was first developed. Before development, Marylebone was open fields used for hunting. Marylebone Lane and its continuation, Marylebone High Street follow the route of a country lane that meandered through the fields.

Location:	Oxford St, W1. North side of the street
Map grid:	3b
Tube station:	Bond Street or Marble Arch
Bus route:	6, 7, 10, 12, 15, 23, 30, 73, 94, 98, 137, 159, 274
Architect:	R. F. Atkinson, Daniel Burnham and others. Clock by Gilbert Bayes
Built:	1907–28
Style:	Classical
Cryptic clue:	Retailing a variety of items, not just refrigerators

Selfridges, 400 Oxford Street, W1

If you fancied a cup of tea followed by an afternoon of shooting, then Selfridge's was the place to go. Selfridge's was a store unlike anything in England when it opened. It revolutionized retailing, with services such as a library and silence room, first aid ward, bureau de change, a savings bank and a rooftop tea garden with rifle range attached.

American Gordon Selfridge excelled at marketing his store. When French aviateur Louis Bleriot made the first aeroplane flight across the English Channel, Mr Selfridge drove to Dover to meet the pilot and persuaded him to rent the aircraft for a few days. The plane was transported by rail to London the same day and installed in the basement of Selfridges, ready for customers to view from 9am the next morning.

The 'Queen of Time' stands majestically below the clock.

Mayfair, Piccadilly & St James's

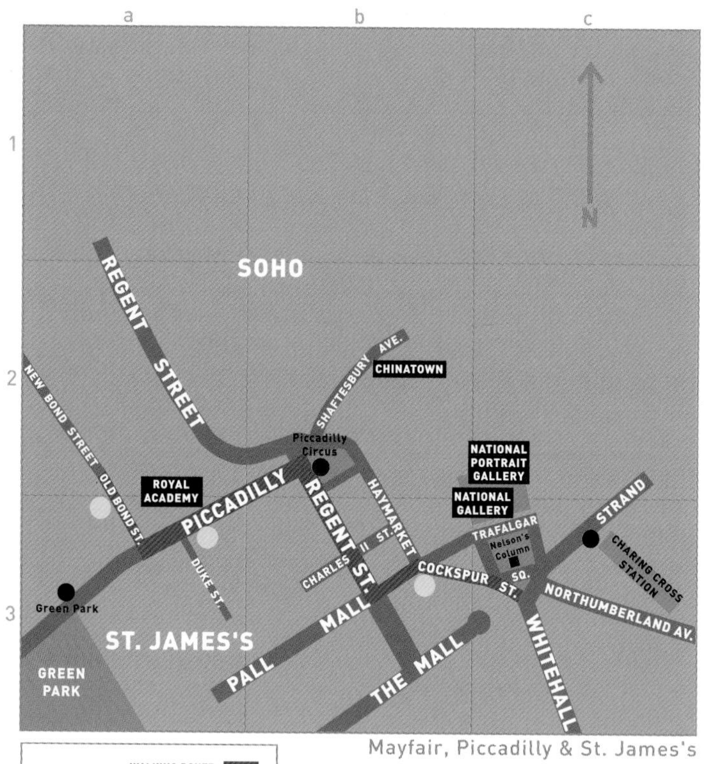

Mayfair, Piccadilly & St. James's

Location:	Old Bond St, W1. West side of the street
Map grid:	3a
Tube station:	Piccadilly Circus or Green Park
Bus route:	8, 9, 14, 19, 22, 38
Architect:	Unknown
Built:	1879
Style:	Classical influences
Cryptic clue:	Elderly Agent 007

Royal Arcade, 28 Old Bond Street, W1

Shopping arcades were the height of fashion in the 18th and 19th centuries, attracting well-heeled customers to shop with leisure in the covered corridors. Walking through an arcade today one enters a time capsule of retailing, with specialized shops serving customers in quiet and intimate surroundings. Burlington Arcade, near to the Royal Arcade, has a beadle in uniform to enforce 18th century laws governing behaviour in the arcade. The laws prohibit singing, whistling, running and the carrying of open umbrellas onto the premises.

The Royal Arcade, originally called 'The Arcade' was distinguished by the Royal title in 1882 after Queen Victoria bought goods there. It was built to link Albermarle Street and the luxurious Browns Hotel, to the shops in Bond Street.

Bond Street was named after Thomas Bond, the Comptroller of the Household to Queen Henrietta Maria, widow of King Charles I. Bond bought the land and laid out the street in 1686. It was extended through open fields to Oxford Street in 1721.

Location:	Piccadilly, SW1. South side of the street
Map grid:	3a
Tube station:	Piccadilly Circus or Green Park
Bus route:	8, 9, 14, 19, 22, 38
Architect:	Wimperis, Simpson & Guthrie
Built:	1926–7
Style:	Georgian
Cryptic clue:	Department store named after two gentlemen. Is one a builder working with stone?

Fortnum & Mason, 181 Piccadilly, SW1

Fortnum & Mason was designed to look old fashioned on the exterior, but inside it was a modern department store.

William Fortnum was a footman in the household of Queen Anne in 1707. One of his daily chores was to change the candles throughout the Royal Household. Sensing an opportunity, he sought permission to keep the candle ends and then made a profit by selling them to colleagues. With the extra income, William Fortnum's dreams of running a grocery shop were realized when he went into business with Hugh Mason.

If you walk by Fortnum & Mason as the clock strikes the hour, look up from Piccadilly at the building's ornate clock. You will see mechanical models of Mr Fortnum and Mr Mason in 18th century costume emerge to the sound of chimes and bow to each other. Like the building itself, the clock appears to be from another century but it was made in 1964.

Location:	Cockspur St, SW1. South side of the street
Map grid:	3b
Tube station:	Piccadilly Circus or Charing Cross
Bus route:	3, 6, 9, 11, 12, 13, 15, 23, 24, 53, 77a, 88, 91, 139, 159
Architect:	A.T. Boulton
Built:	1906–7
Style:	Baroque influences
Cryptic clue:	Keeping money safe north of the border

Bank of Scotland, 14–16 Cockspur St SW1

Walk through the ornate doorway in the photograph and you may feel as though you have stepped back in time. The premises are now a banking hall for the Bank of Scotland but originally they served as the ticketing office of the Hamburg–America Steamship Line. Original artefacts have been retained: wall paintings with shipping themes, and an elaborate multi-faced clock that shows local times in the ports of Calcutta, Yokohama, Port Said, Bombay, Sydney and Hong Kong. The decorations suggest an era before the romance of travel was lost.

The Latin phrase above the door *Quis separabit* means 'Who shall separate us?'

Cockspur Street was first recorded as Cock Spurr Street in 1753. It was the place to purchase spurs for fighting cocks that competed at the cockpit in nearby Whitehall.

Westminster & Victoria

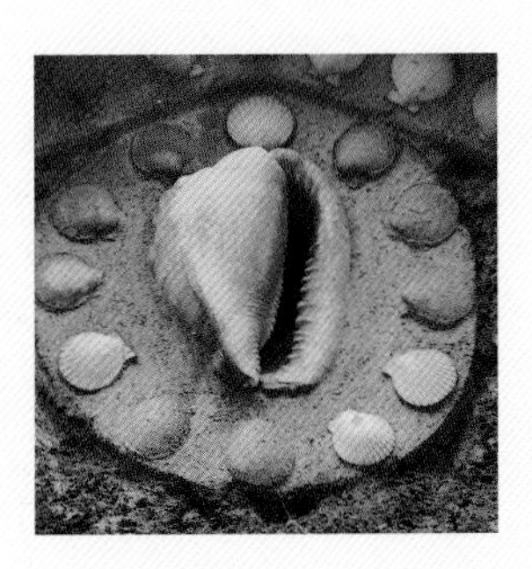

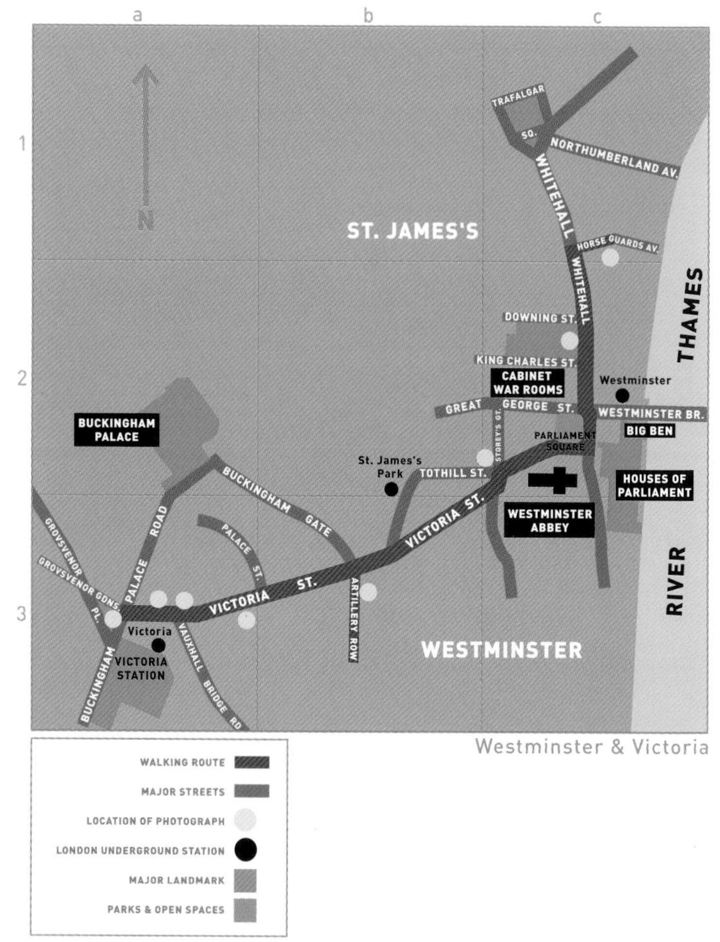

Westminster & Victoria

Location:	Horse Guards Ave, SW1. West side of the street
Map grid:	1c
Tube station:	Westminster or Charing Cross
Bus route:	3, 11, 12, 24, 53, 77a, 88, 159
Architect:	E.Vincent Harris. Statues by Charles Wheeler
Built:	1930s to 1950s
Style:	Classical
Cryptic clue:	The ministerial lady lies in a defensive position

Ministry of Defence, Horse Guards Avenue, SW1

This magnificent lady represents Water. She has a twin called Earth who reclines on the opposite wall. Original plans envisaged four statues to symbolize the elements, but post-war spending cutbacks halted the completion of Fire and Air.

The Ministry of Defence was built on the site of the Royal Palace of Whitehall. During the Ministry's construction, King Henry VIII's wine cellar was discovered. It was 70 feet long and 30 feet wide. The cellar's location was a problem. In short, it was in the way. After consultation with engineers, an ingenious solution was suggested. The cellar was encased in concrete, lifted a few feet and laid in a new location. Once that was complete, construction of the Ministry continued above the cellar.

Public access to the cellar is limited to an occasional open day, by prior arrangement.

Location: Whitehall, SW1. West side of the street
Map grid: 2c
Tube station: Westminster
Bus route: 3, 11, 12, 24, 53, 77a, 88, 159
Architect: Gilbert Scott
Built: 1868–73
Style: Italian Renaissance
Cryptic clue: Where government overseas diplomacy is fashioned

Foreign Office, Whitehall, SW1

Looking at this splendid building, it is hard to imagine that only 40 years ago there were calls to replace it. Its faded grandeur and changing tastes conspired in calls to demolish the Victorian gem. A public outcry succeeded in saving it though, and it now has the distinction of Grade I Listed Building status, protecting it for the future.

Architect Gilbert Scott's initial designs for the Foreign Office were Gothic. His masterpieces, St Pancras railway station hotel and the Albert Memorial, confirmed his preference for the Gothic style. Gothic, however, did not suit Prime Minister Lord Palmerston's idea of grandeur. For the Foreign Office, at the centre of a huge Empire, he demanded a commanding and majestic edifice. Whatever the design, it had to send a visual signal of Britain's mighty position in the world. Lord Palmerston favoured Italianate and his wishes prevailed.

Location:	Storey's Gate, SW1. West side of the street
Map grid:	2c
Tube station:	St James's or Westminster
Bus route:	3, 11, 12, 24, 53, 77a, 88, 159
Architect:	H.V. Lanchester & E.A. Rickards. Sculptures by Henry Poole
Built:	1905–11
Style:	Edwardian Baroque
Cryptic clue:	A hall where John Wesley's brethren meet

Methodist Central Hall, Storey's Gate, SW1

If the walls of Methodist Central Hall could talk they would speak of heroes and history. Twentieth century icons have delivered passionate speeches here, and events of major historical import echo in its corridors. Methodist Central Hall hosted the inaugural General Assembly of the United Nations in 1946; wartime Prime Minister Winston Churchill opened a speech there in 1945 with the words 'Victory is certain, victory is near'; exiled French General Charles De Gaulle announced the Free French movement in 1940. Earlier, Indian independence campaigner Mahatma Ghandi addressed a Temperance Society meeting in 1931; and Suffragettes gathered in 1914 to demand the vote for women.

Cryptic clue explanation: John Wesley founded the Methodist Church.

Location:	Artillery Row, S.W.1. East side of the street
Map grid:	3b
Tube station:	Victoria or St James's Park
Bus route:	11, 24, 507
Architect:	C.J.C. Pawley
Built:	1897
Style:	Queen Anne
Cryptic clue:	The Army & Navy can gaze upon this naked maiden

Westminster Palace Gardens, Artillery Row, SW1

Victorian clothing was designed to conceal the skin. The term 'buttoned up' not only referred to clothing but also to Victorian attitudes regarding public displays of flesh. Even the sight of a woman's ankle made the male heart flutter, and some men would stand at street corners waiting for women to pass by and lift their long skirts, exposing an inch or two of leg as they climbed the pavement. It must have been quite exciting therefore for Victorian men to take a trip to Westminster Palace Gardens and gaze upon the semi-clad maiden in the photograph.

Artillery Row was built on what was a large swathe of open land used for a variety of purposes including artillery practice.

Cryptic clue explanation: Army & Navy is a department store next to Westminster Palace Gardens.

Location:	Victoria St, SW1. South side of the street
Map grid:	3a
Tube station:	Victoria
Bus route:	2, 8, 11, 16, 24, 36, 38, 52, 73, 82, 239, 507, C1, C10
Architect:	John Frances Bentley
Built:	1895–1903
Style:	A mixture of Byzantine and Romanesque
Cryptic clue:	The cathedral, *not* the abbey

Westminster Cathedral, Victoria St SW1

Take a ride in the elevator to the top of Westminster Cathedral's soaring campanile and look towards the river. The area was open land known as Tothill Fields until the 19th century. It had a myriad of uses, including animal grazing, market gardening, and the fighting of duels. From the 12th century , Tothill Fields hosted knights tournaments and later bear and bull baiting.

Westminster Cathedral's architect died before his masterpiece was completed. Even today, some of the stunning mosaics inside are unfinished.

Location:	Victoria St, SW1. North side of the street
Map grid:	3a
Tube station:	Victoria
Bus route:	2, 8, 11, 16, 24, 36, 38, 52, 73, 82, 239, 507, C1, C10
Architect:	Frank Matcham
Built:	1910
Style:	Edwardian Baroque
Cryptic clue:	Theatrical version of a Queen's palatial dwelling

Victoria Palace Theatre, Victoria Street, SW1

Where is Pavlova's statue? The mystery of the disappearing statue has been a puzzle since it was removed from the cupola of the Victoria Palace Theatre in 1940. Prima ballerina Anna Pavlova was among the first performers to appear on-stage at the Victoria Palace Theatre. In honour of this memorable event, the owner, Alfred Butts, commissioned the statue of Pavlova to adorn the roof of his theatre. During the Blitz, it was taken down and placed in storage. It was never seen again.

Location:	Victoria St, SW1. North side of the street
Map grid:	3a
Tube station:	Victoria
Bus route:	2, 8, 11, 16, 24, 36, 38, 52, 73, 82, 239, 507, C1, C10
Architect:	Ron Sidell. Sculptures by Barry Baldwin
Built:	1997
Style:	Cast iron architecture influences
Cryptic clue:	A menagerie by the Queen's theatre

Allington House, 150 Victoria Street, SW1

Jaws had claimed another victim in 1997 when this sculpture was created. The shark's mouth contained a man's head and a boot, cast in stone. The building's tenants were not amused, however, and they paid the sculptor to empty the shark's mouth. It was not the first time a client did not appreciate the artist's visual gags. On a similar work for a German shopping centre, the client hired the sculptor to reduce the size of the orang-utan's over-sized genitals.

Cryptic clue explanation: Allington House is next to the Victoria Palace Theatre.

Location	Lower Grosvenor Gardens, SW1. West side of the garden
Map Grid	3a
Tube station	Victoria
Bus route	2, 8, 11, 16, 24, 36, 38, 52, 73, 82, 239, 507, C1, C10
Architect	Unknown
Built	Unknown
Style	Classical
Cryptic clue	Temple of the lawnmower

Shell Garden Hut, Lower Grosvenor Gardens, SW1

When the Prince Regent, who was later crowned King George IV, fancied a night out, he sometimes caroused in the public houses surrounding what is now Lower Grosvenor Gardens. One pub's name, 'The Bacchanals', was slurred by customers often enough to become known as the 'Bag of Nails'.

The garden hut was built in the Classical Greek Temple style that was so popular in the 18th century.

Hyde Park Corner & Knightsbridge

Hyde Park Corner & Knightsbridge

Location	Grosvenor Place, SW1. West side of the street
Map Grid	2b
Tube station	Hyde Park Corner
Bus route	2, 8, 9, 10, 14, 16, 19, 22, 36, 38, 52, 73, 74, 82, 137
Architect	Albert Richardson. Sculptor unknown
Built	1955
Style	Classical
Cryptic clue	Overlooking the Palace's back garden

33 Grosvenor Place, SW1

No wonder King George III was mad: a row of houses that looked directly into his back garden had been built on Grosvenor Place. The garden in question was attached to Buckingham Palace and in 1767 the King petitioned Parliament for money to buy the land on Grosvenor Place and stop the housing project. Parliament refused his request and development spread around the Palace perimeter.

The King's neighbours included the patients of the Lock Hospital built on what is now 33 Grosvenor Place. Its mission was to care for females 'suffering from disorders contracted by a vicious course of life'.

The significance of the sculpture in the photograph is unknown. In addition to the rooftop art, there are gargoyles on the building's facade. They depict the Angel of Light overcoming the Power of Darkness, a suitable allegory because the building's first tenant was the Association of Electrical Industries.

Location	Hyde Park Corner, SW1
Map grid	2b
Tube station	Hyde Park Corner
Bus route	2, 8, 9, 10, 14, 16, 19, 22, 36, 38, 52, 73, 74, 82, 137
Architect	Decimus Burton. Sculpture by Adrian Jones
Built	1827–8. Sculpture: 1912
Style	Corinthian Triumphal Arch
Cryptic clue	A saucy rubber boot

Wellington Arch, Hyde Park Corner, SW1

If the Iron Duke had not been victorious in his military campaigns, this triumphal arch might have been called the Napoleon Arch. 'Iron Duke' was the nickname of the Duke of Wellington, Commander of the British Army that vanquished Napoleon's forces during the Battle of Waterloo in 1815.

Wellington lived at Apsley House, Hyde Park Corner. Letters addressed to Number One, London will be delivered to Apsley House. It earned its unique address because it was the first building seen by visitors travelling into London through a nearby tollgate.

The group of statues on Wellington Arch is called 'Peace in a Quadriga' and represents Peace descending from heaven into the chariot of war.

Cryptic clue explanation:
in Britain, rubber boots are known as 'Wellingtons'.

Location	Piccadilly, W1. North side of the street
Map grid	1b
Tube station	Hyde Park Corner
Bus route	2, 8, 9, 10, 14, 16, 19, 22, 36, 38, 52, 73, 74, 82, 137
Architect	Thomas Colcutt and Stanley Hamp
Built	1907
Style	Edwardian Baroque
Cryptic clue	A tough musical place to eat

Gloucester House 149 Old Park Lane, W1

It is appropriate that the building in the photograph houses the Hard Rock Cafe, because another hard rock features in the history of this location. Lord Elgin and his infamous marbles are associated with 149 Old Park Lane – it was the site of his townhouse. The marbles in question are ancient Greek sculptures, friezes and columns removed by Elgin in questionable circumstances from the Parthenon in Athens. When the treasures arrived in London at the beginning of the 19th century they were stored at Elgin's house and eventually sold to the British Government for a significant sum. They are among the most popular exhibits at the British Museum. Successive Greek governments have requested their return, to no avail.